YOU CAN TEACH YOURSELF®
PAN FLUTE

By Costel Puscoiu

D0923876

CD Contents

1 Merrily We Roll Along [:31]
2 Au Claire de la Lune [:30]
3 Little Waltz [:36]
4 Barcarolle [:33]
5 Theme (from *New World Symphony*) [:33]
6 To Joy [:48]
7 Jingle Bells [:36]
8 The Green Leave of the Jasmine [:45]
9 Children's Song [:38]
10 Frere Jacques [:47]
11 The Pony [1:07]
12 Fanfare [:23]
13 We Walk and Sing the Carols [:39]
14 Lullaby for Christmas [1:01]
15 Little Brown Jug [:36]
16 Down Below in Bethlehem [:43]
17 The First Nowell [:39]
18 March [:43]
19 Little Rabbit [:23]
20 Be Quiet Now [:41]
21 Air [:49]
22 Hopping [:33]
23 Oh, Susanna [1:01]
24 When the Saints Go Marching In [:27]
25 Auld Lang Syne [1:01]
26 Dance from Brebu [:43]
27 A Child is Born [:41]

28 Fox, You Stole the Goose [:28]
29 Theme (from *Swanlake*) [:40]
30 Shepherd, Shepherd [:36]
31 Thus the Good People Drink [:43]
32 Angels and Shepherds [:33]
33 Scarborough Fair [:40]
34 God Rest Ye Merry Gentlemen [:52]
35 Aura Lee [:50]
36 Melody (from *Album for the Youth*) [:48]
37 Rondino [1:01]
38 Greensleeves [1:33]
39 Romance [1:07]
40 Musz I Denn [:36]
41 London Bridge is Falling Down [:35]
42 Song of the Volga Boatmen [1:34]
43 Gavotte [:58]
44 Merry Widow Waltz [:47]
45 Finale (from Symphony no. 1) [:52]
46 Theme (from *Eine kleine Nachtmusik*) [:28]
47 Burlesque (from *Music Book for Wolfgang*) [:44]
48 Andante [:43]
49 I Have a Coin [:54]
50 Rondeau [:25]
51 Tambourin [:57]
52 Gavotte [:39]
53 Can-Can [:26]

54 German Dance [:33]
55 Minuet [:33]
56 Martial Air [:46]
57 Galoppa, Galoppa [1:05]
58 Theme (from *Moldavia*) [:31]
59 Gloria in Excelsis Deo [:58]
60 Hark! The Herald Angels Sing [1:08]
61 Long, Long Ago [:47]
62 Melody (from *Scheherazade*) [:39]
63 Michael's Song [:54]
64 Barbu the Fiddler [:49]
65 The Yellow Rose of Texas [:31]
66 When I Was on Ialomita [:35]
67 Father Christmas [1:18]
68 Silent Night [1:04]
69 March (from *Judas Maccabaeus*) [1:04]
70 Lullaby [:53]
71 Amazing Grace [:47]
72 Etude [1:24]
73 Theme (from Symphony no. 40) [:38]
74 Three-leaved Clover [1:01]
75 Gavotte [:41]
76 Early French Song [1:15]
77 Pavane [1:10]
78 Andante (from Violin Concerto) [1:23]
79 Air (from Opera *The Magic Flute*) [:42]

Young pan flutist (Mihai Puscoiu)

Contents

About the Author

Costel Puscoiu was born on August 29, 1951, in Bucharest, Romania. He studied and graduated at the "Ciprian Porumbescu" College of Music in Bucharest, majoring in "Composition and Theory". In Romania he worked as a music teacher, and for some years he was a conductor and researcher at the Institute for Ethnocology and Folklore in Bucharest. He was also a member of the Society of Romanian Composers.

His compositions comprise symphonic music (symphony, cantatas, concerto for viola), chamber music (string quartets, sonata for clarinet and piano, contemporary for several ensembles, pieces of music for pan flute), choir pieces, and filmscores. His hand has also appeared in several musicological and folkloristic studies and articles.

In September of 1982 he preferred The Netherlands to his native Romania; now he's working in the music-school department as a pan flute teacher and a leader of an orchestra at "The Free Academy Westvest" in Delft. Meanwhile he has become a member of the Dutch Composers Association.

Introduction

The increasing interest in the pan flute made me decide to write this book, YOU CAN TEACH YOURSELF® PAN FLUTE, for studying this fine instrument, based on my practice of teaching.

My wish is that this book will help to take the pan flute to a higher level equal to that of other classical instruments. Then we can leave behind us the period when the pan flute was used only to play Romanian and South American folk music.

This book contains theoretical explanations, because only a good understanding of theory can lead an instrumentalist onto a good course. In practice, working with my book, the pan flute player will learn to know and appreciate music in general and to perform music with pleasure.

This book is written for a pan flute with 12 pipes, tuned in C major, but can also be used for learning to play pan flutes of another tone range, with different pitches and of different materials, because the basic techniques remain the same on all pan flutes.

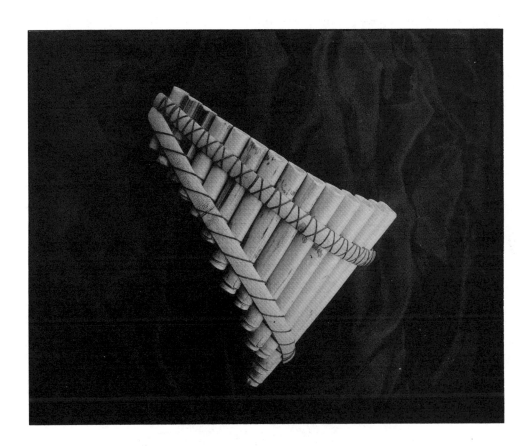

Short History of the Pan Flute

In my opinion the pan flute is one of the finest and oldest musical instruments in the world. It is difficult to say when, where and in which form the instrument first appeared, because there is little material evidence.

I think the pan flute is so old because it is so simple. It was probably preceded only by percussion instruments. After primitive man produced sound by hitting things, he probably accidentally discovered sound production by blowing a pipe: stems of plants (reed or bamboo) or animal bones.

The **"one-pipe pan flute"** probably came first. Man in his development started to distinguish between different pitches and to make instruments which could produce tones. The first step in the pan flute's development therefore was joining one pipe to another. The rest was easy: one pipe next to the other. There were also variations in form: straight (raft-shaped), slightly bent, or bundled.

The best-known legend about the birth of the pan flute centers around the **shepherd god Pan** and the **nymph Syrinx**. Pan is a creature half human, half animal, goat-footed and with horns, who roams the forests solitarily. At his appearance, which is usually sudden, he causes "panic" because of his mischievous tricks. When Pan met the beautiful Syrinx he fell in love with her at once. Not interested in his advances she fled to the water's edge, Pan at her heels, and appealed to the supreme god, Zeus, for help. Zeus helped by turning Syrinx into a reed, and then there was nothing for Pan to do but cut and bundle this reed and give voice to his pangs of love on the pan flute thus formed.

The pan flute has in different times and geographical zones had different names: **syrinx** (Greece), **fistula** (Old Roman), **p'ai hsiao** (China), **frestel** (France-Middle Age), **nai, muscal** and **tevnita** (Romania), **antara, hauyra, puhura, siku** and **rondador** (South America).

The pan flute can have a varying amount of pipes from 5 to 34 in one row (a), two rows (b) or in a bundle (c). The shape in a straight line is characteristic of the South American pan flutes. The curved shape belongs specifically to the Romanian pan flute.

a

b

or

c

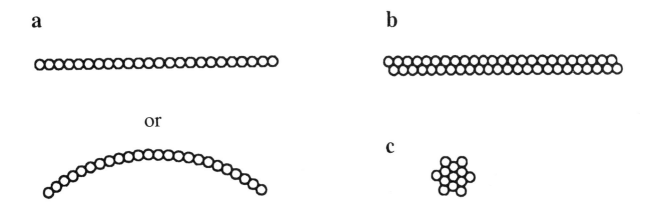

The pan flutes are usually made from bamboo, wood or synthetic material, and very often from paper, ceramics, glass or crystal.

The tone quality of the Romanian bamboo pan flute best fulfills the demands modern concert audiences make on a musical instrument.

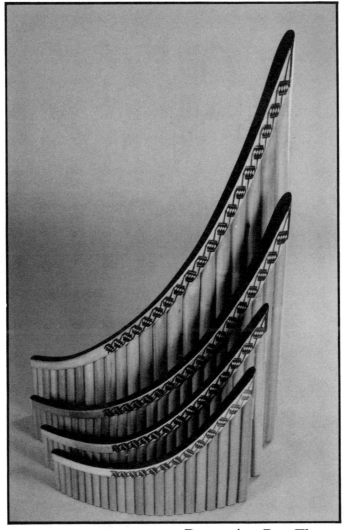

Romanian Pan Flutes

The pan flute revival came about after World War II through the effects of **Fânica Luca**, the famous pan flute player who performed at the world exhibitions of 1937 (Paris) and 1939 (New York). He did many concert tours in France, England, Poland, Egypt, China, Russia and the United States. In 1949, aided by the Institute of Folklore Research in Bukarest, he started a pan flute class, which in 1953 moved to the Music Lyceum. The results of his hard work were grand, and after the '70s a generation of fantastic pan flute players appeared in the West. Exponents of this school are: **Gheorghe Zamfir, Damian Luca, Simion Stanciu, Nicolae Pîrvu, Constantin Dobre, Radu Simion, Damian Cîrlanaru** and others.

Gheorghe Zamfir has the most qualities, and he has seized every opportunity to become the most well-known pan flute player in the world. Everywhere he is the world's best-known ambassador of Romanian folk music, and he has perfected the pan flute technique to a very high level. Gheorghe Zamfir has made millions of records and CDs of mainly Romanian folk music, but also of light music and classical music. With his magic sound, his incredible virtuosity and his inimitable doinas, he has managed to beguile all music lovers. That is why his name is rightly linked to the pan flute.

Simion Stanciu "Syrinx" helped to make the pan flute better known thanks to his virtuoso technique and his magnificent performances of famous classical works. During the past 10 years he has given a large number of concerts and made a great many recordings (CD and vinyl) of classical music only. All specialists and music lovers who listen to Simion Stanciu, whom musicologists have called "the master of the classical pan flute" and "the Paganini of the pan flute", have to admit that the pan flute should be regarded as a true "classical" instrument.

Basic Music Notation
Notes

This is a note:

A note has three parts: The head

The stem

The flag

Staff

Notes are written on the five-line staff:

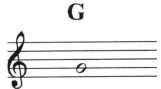

Clef

At the beginning of each staff is written a clef. The **treble clef** begins on the second line of the staff with a curl. This is the note **G**:

G

Notes may be placed in the staff, above the staff and below the staff:

Names of the Notes

A note will bear the name of the line or space it occupies on the staff. The notes are named after the following letters: **A, B, C, D, E, F, G**. The location of a note in, above, or below the staff will indicate the pitch (height or depth of a note).

Types of Notes

The type of a note will indicate the length of its sound.

𝑜   This is a whole note. The head is hollow. It does not have a stem.
A whole note will receive **four beats** or counts.

This is a half note. The head is hollow. It has a stem.
A half note will receive **two beats** or counts.

This is a quarter note. The head is solid. It has a stem.
A quarter note will receive **one beat** or count.

or   These are eighth notes. The head is solid. It has a stem and a flag.
An eighth note will receive **1/2 beat** or count (two for one beat).

or 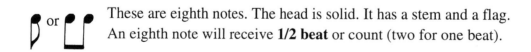   These are **sixteenth notes**. The head is solid. It has a stem and two flags.
A sixteenth note will receive **1/4 beat** or count (four for one beat).
Two sixteenth notes are equal to an eighth note, and four sixteenths are equal to a quarter note.

Rests

A **rest** is a sign used to designate a period of measured silence. This period of silence will be of the same duration of time as the note to which it corresponds.

 This is a whole rest. Note that it hangs down from the line.
A whole rest will receive **four beats** or counts.

 This is a half rest. Note that it lies on the line.
A half rest will receive **two beats** or counts.

 This is a quarter rest. A quarter rest will receive **one beat** or count.

This is an eighth rest. An eighth rest will receive **1/2 beat** or count.

This is a sixteenth rest. A sixteenth rest will receive **1/4 beat** or count.

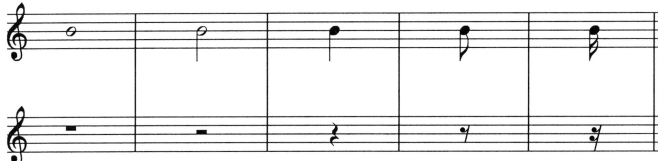

Dotted Notes

The most common dotted notes are the dotted half note and the dotted quarter note.

 This is a dotted half note.
A dotted half note will receive **three beats** or counts.

 This is a dotted quarter note.
A dotted quarter note will receive **one and a half beats** or counts.

 This is a dotted eighth note.
A dotted eighth note will receive **three quarter beats** or counts.

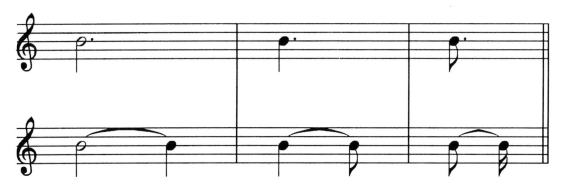

Measure

Measures help us to read music more easily. Measure bars have an equal number of beats and are limited by **bar lines**. The end of a piece of music is shown by a **double bar**.

The Time Signature

Each piece of music begins with a time signature:

4
4
The top number indicates the number of beats per measure. (4 beats per measure).

The bottom number indicates the type of note receiving one beat per measure (a quarter note receives one beat).

2
4
2 beats per measure.
A quarter note receives one beat.

3
4
3 beats per measure.
A quarter note receives one beat.

6
8
6 beats per measure.
An eighth note receives one beat.

C   Is the same as a 4/4 time signature.

Tempo Signs

The tempo signs indicate how fast or slow we must play. The most common are Italian words:

Largo	= very slow
Andante	= slow
Andantino	= moderately slow
Moderato	= moderately
Allegretto	= moderately fast
Allegro	= fast
Presto	= very fast

Dynamics

The dynamics are signs for musical expression and are also Italian terms. They indicate when we must play softly or loudly.

pp	= pianissimo	= very soft
p	= piano	= soft
mp	= mezzo piano	= moderately soft
mf	= mezzo forte	= moderately loud
f	= forte	= loud
ff	= fortissimo	= very loud
◁	= crescendo	= gradually get louder
▷	= decrescendo	= gradually get softer

Other Basic Music Signs

‖: :‖ = **Repeat sign**. When they are written, repeat the music found between the signs.

Da Capo al Fine = When that is written, repeat the music from the beginning to the word **Fine**.

 = **A pickup** occurs if a music piece begins with an incomplete measure. A pickup note may be only one note or a group of notes appearing before the actual start of the piece. They serve to lead into the melody.

 = **The tie** is a curved line that connects two notes of the same pitch. When a tie occurs, play the first note and hold (do not tongue) the second note.

 = **The slur** is a curved line connecting two or more notes of a different pitch. When a slur occurs, tongue only the first note.

 = **Fermata**. It means to hold the note extra long.

 = **Endings**. Sometimes in a song there appears a first and second ending. Take the first ending and observe the repeat sign. Then, on the second time through, skip the first ending, play the second ending, and continue on with the music.

♯ = A **sharp** raises the pitch of a note one half step.

♭ = A **flat** lowers the pitch of a note one half step.

♮ = **Natural sign**. All sharps or flats are cancelled by a natural sign. When a sharp or a flat sign appears in a measure, all remaining notes in that measure of that particular pitch remain sharped or flatted unless a natural sign cancels the sharp or flat.

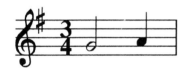 = The **key signature** will appear at the beginning of a music piece. It will show whether there are sharps or flats in a song. If a sharp or flat appears, all notes of that pitch are sharped or flatted unless cancelled by a natural sign.

3 = **The triplet** is a group of three notes (eighths) played in the time of two notes (eighths) of the same kind. An eighth triplet is equal in time value to a quarter or two eighths.

The Pan Flute

A small pan flute is an ideal instrument on which to begin. Later when you have progressed in ability, you might consider the purchase of a larger pan flute.

The real tone range of our pan flute with 12 pipes is between **c2** and **g3**, and **the notation is c1** to **g2** in the treble clef, one octave lower. This pan flute is **tuned** in **C major** (with f).

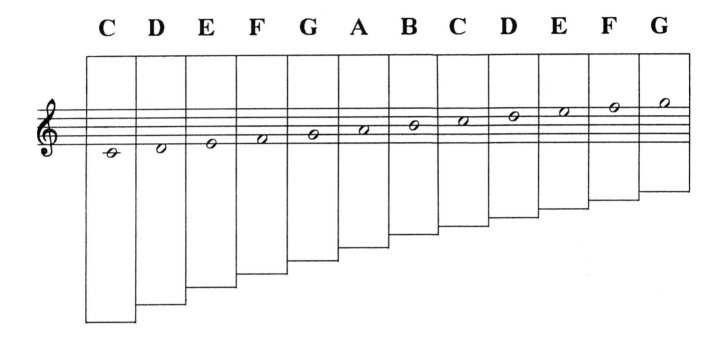

The bamboo pipes are open at the top and closed at the bottom. The pipes are positioned in a concave row with the longest pipes on the right, running down evenly to the shortest pipe on the left. The pipes are tuned with beeswax.

The instrument is played holding the hollow side to the mouth, and the longest pipe in the right hand.

All pan flutes need maintenance and must not be exposed to high extremes in temperature. It is recommended to clean the pipes with a (recorder) swab, before and after each time the pan flute is used. The salts and acids have a bad effect on the instrument. The interior of some bamboo or wood pan flutes must be rubbed regularly with almond oil. This is also done with a lint-free swab.

If a player should have any problem with the pitch or a deficiency of his pan flute I strongly advise him to consult his teacher, the maker of the instrument or the person who sold it to him, because the pan flute is a precision instrument and also quite delicate.

How to Learn a New Piece of Music

1. Look at the time signature. How many beats are there per measure ?

2. Clap the rhythm while you count the note values out loud.

Example:

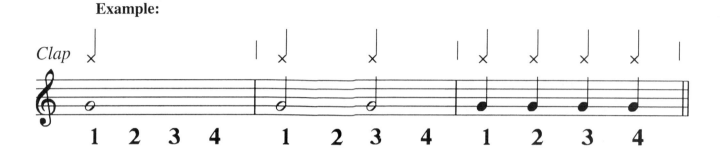

3. Play the notes on your pan flute.

How to Practice

The possible result depends on several factors, but in particular on the qualities of the student and the time he or she spends practicing. Regularity in study, which means a certain amount of practice every day, is very important, because music, just like sport, demands a daily training.

Every true instrumentalist, whether amateur or professional, needs to have a fixed **study program**. Start with 10 - 15 minutes. After a few weeks you can play 30 minutes or more.

The pan flute can be played solo (in the beginning that is the best way to practice) but also accompanied by other instruments or in ensembles. The pan flute sounds good when accompanied by chord instruments like piano, organ, harp or guitar and in folk music, by accordion or cymbal.

The pan flute player can belong to several instrumental groupings as a soloist or a member of an orchestra. The instrument goes together well with violin, cymbal, accordion and bass in specific Romanian folklore ensembles, but it can join in popular music groups as well.

How to Hold the Pan Flute

One could guess from the instrument's curve that we hold the tip of the longest pipes in the right hand. The lowest tone is to the player's right.

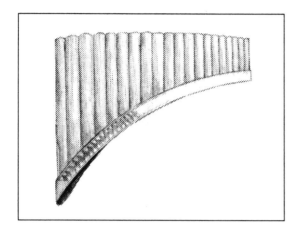 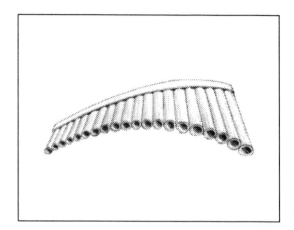

Position of the right hand

The bent middle finger of the right hand holds the pan flute under the rim; ring finger and little finger support the middle finger by curving around the tip. By leaning on the rim the index finger takes care of the straight vertical position. The thumb with its "cushion" at the instrument's side or back gives support to the pan flute.

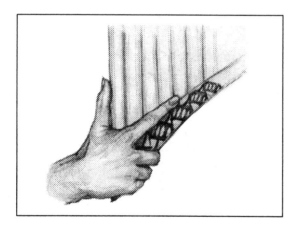 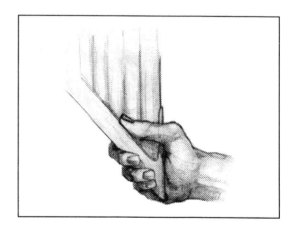

Position of the left hand

The tip of the left middle finger is placed high up on a pipe, the tip of the little finger is on the lower rim. The cushions of the index and ring fingers are simply placed on the instrument. The palm of the left hand does not touch the pan flute at all.

 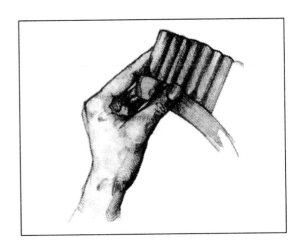

Posture of the body

With a view to the most practical posture, standing up is preferable to sitting down. The feet are placed slightly apart, about straight under the shoulders. The back is somewhat arched and the head is straight. The arms hang down from relaxed shoulders, not touching the trunk, because it will be possible to move the hands freely that hold the bottom of the instrument.

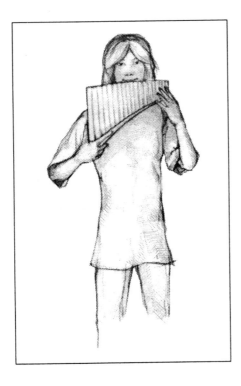 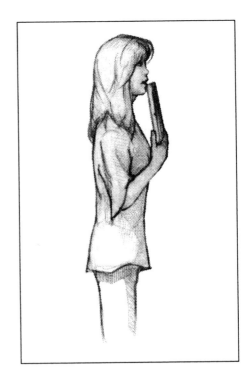

Position of the pan flute to the mouth

While in movement the instrument is held utterly vertical with its upper side to the lower lip of the normally closed mouth, exactly there where the pink part of the lip begins. In movement the pan flute must also be held in a straight horizontal position, because then each pipe will come to the mouth in the same position as the previous one. It goes without saying that any pressure of the instrument on the mouth should be minimal.

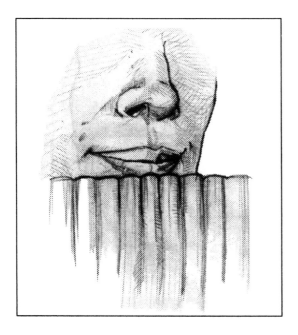 

How to Play the Pan Flute

Embouchure

Embouchure is popularly called the position of the lips while playing. Acquiring a good, small and strong embouchure begins with a smile. With a closed mouth in this position the lips touch the teeth and the corners of the mouth are pulled slightly outward. So, close your mouth, squeeze your lips tightly, make them touch your teeth, and draw the corners of your mouth slightly outward. Now bring the middle of a pipe (somewhere in the middle of the pan flute) to your lower lip at the correct height and let a current of air open your lips a little, basically like voicing a powerful, non-ending "p". The air streaming out makes a narrow, cleft-shaped opening between the lips, so that the air column reaches the back of the pipe, is divided and produces your first tone.

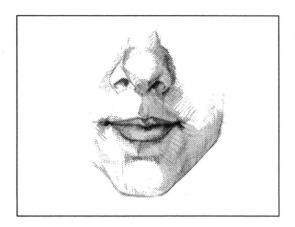 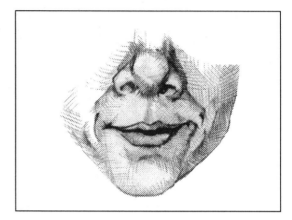

Function of the tongue

The function of the tongue, which is starting off tones, is easy to learn. Start a tone off with "p" and then close the opening between the lips with the tip of the tongue to the upper lip. Drawing back the tip of the tongue is the start of a new tone. Repeat this many times, as much as necessary.

preparation   starting a tone

Movement

The pan flute's horizontal movements to the left and to the right are made with the hands. The hands move in a flowing and synchronous gesture. The essential movement is that of the hands. There can be an auxiliary movement of the head.

Always start at the correct posture for playing, from feet to hands and embouchure, preferably in front of a mirror. The posture in which you can stand in a relaxed way is your best personal posture.

Breathing

Breathing in

The diaphragm is the great respiratory muscle, which must be stimulated by trained abdominal muscles. When breathing in through nose and mouth at the same time the abdominal muscles are relaxed. Store the incoming air as low as possible and do not raise your shoulders. Filling and inflating the chest flattens the diaphragm, which causes the abdominal wall and the ribs to stand out.

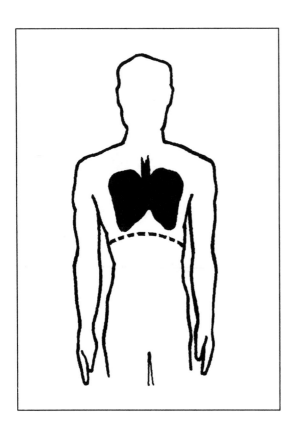 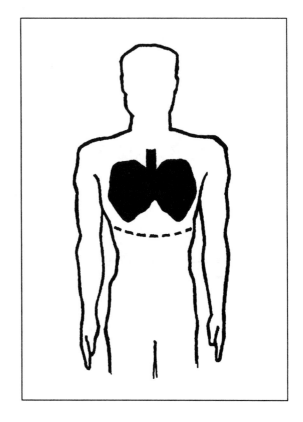

Breathing out

When breathing out one must hold one's chest in an inflated position as long as possible. Controlling the stored air with the tension that is set on the abdominal muscles in between breathing in and out, is called breath support. To use breathing out effectively for playing the pan flute one should not blow powerfully, but instead restrain the muscles of the abdomen and the diaphragm with strength. Breathe in before the last reserve of air held by the abdominal muscles must be used.

Practice breathing and relaxation exercises daily in your spare time. Lying on your back on a flat surface it is impossible to make the frequent mistake of hunching your shoulders.

The internationally recognized signs for breathing (at the recommended place) are: ❜ or ⱽ. In this book I use the first sign, the comma: ❜.

Our First Note: G

G

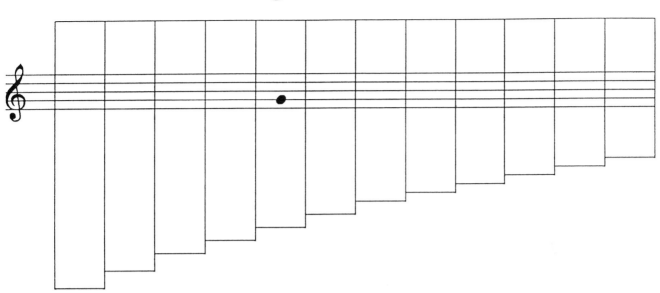

Studies

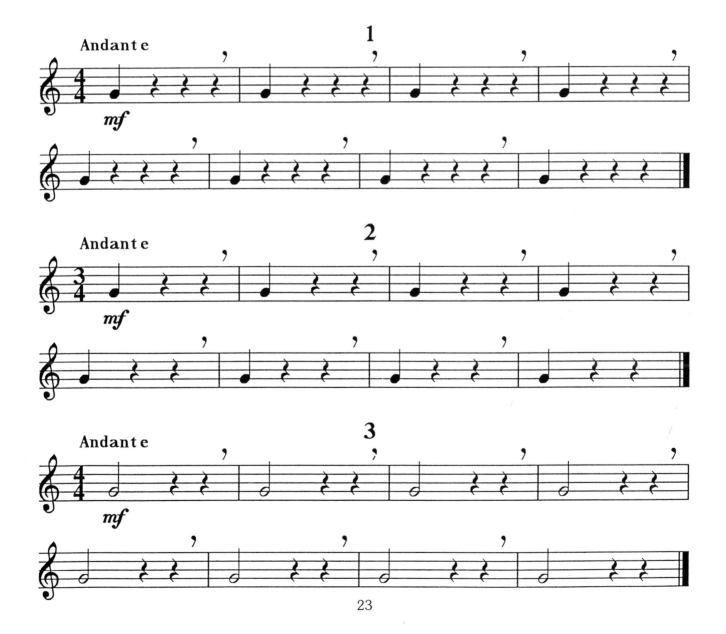

C, D, E and F

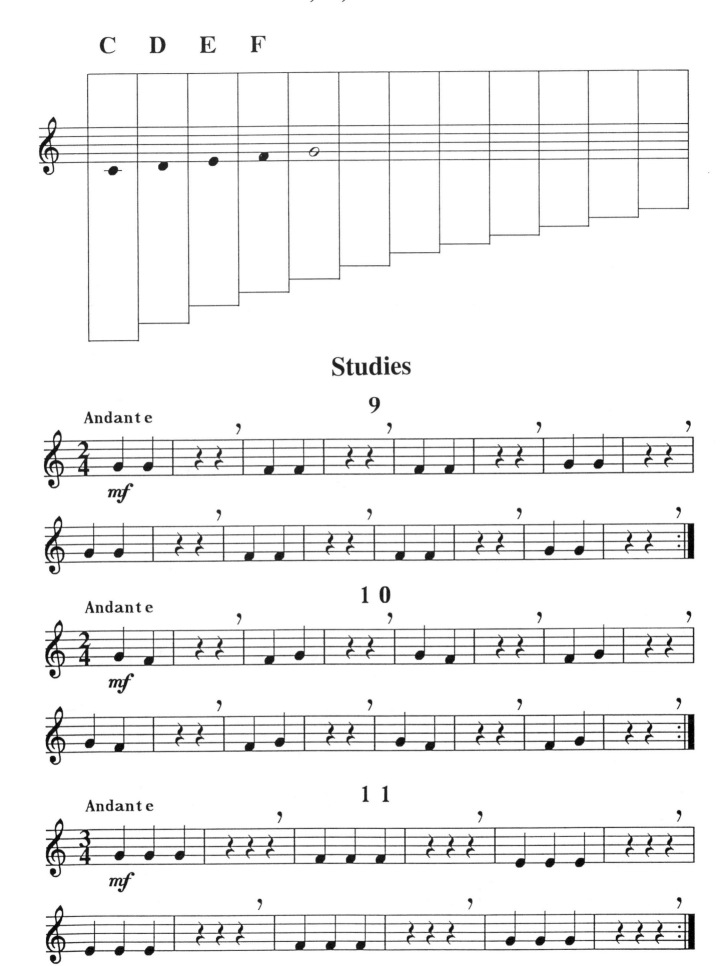

Studies

9

Andante

10

Andante

11

Andante

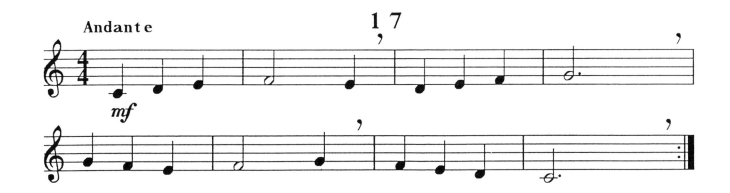

Songs

Merrily We Roll Along

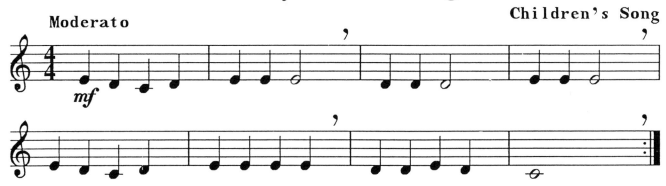

Children's Song

Au Clair de la Lune

French Children's Song

Little Waltz

C. Puscoiu

Barcarolle

Theme
(from "New World Symphony")

To Joy
(from Symphony no. 9)

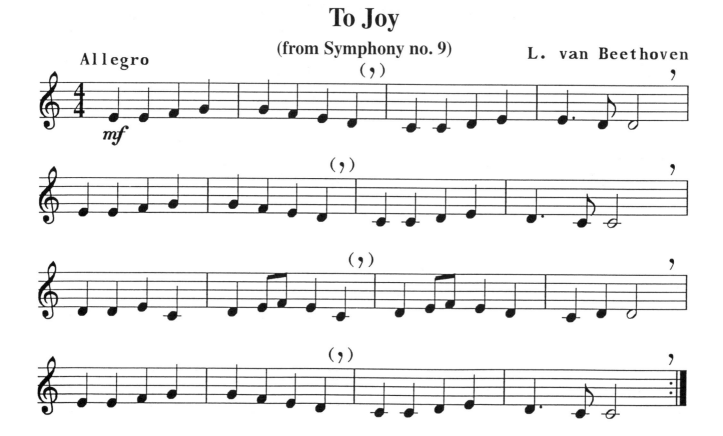

Jingle Bells

Christmas Carol

The Green Leave of the Jasmine

Romanian Folk Song

Intervals: the Second

Playing intervals is part of the basic technique of every musical instrument. Intervals must be studied from the smallest and simplest to the largest and technically most difficult.

On a pan flute playing intervals is harder than on other classical instruments. This is because to play intervals the instrument itself has to move.

A, B and high C

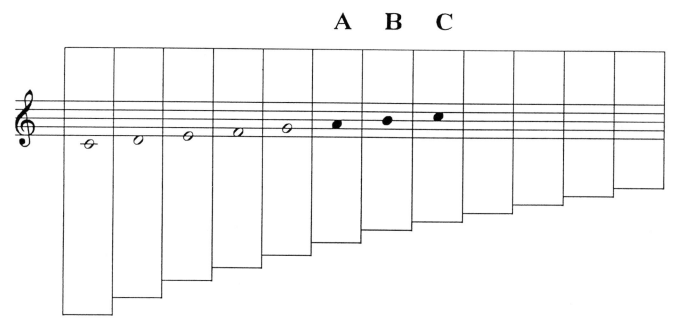

Studies

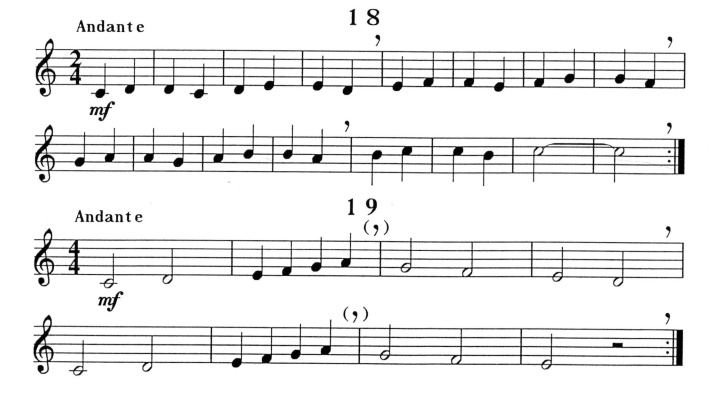

20

Moderato

mf

Fine

D.C. al Fine

21

Moderato

mf

24

Songs
Children's Song

W.A. Mozart

Frere Jacques

Children's Song

The Pony

C. Puscoiu

Fanfare

M. Corrette

We Walk and Sing the Carols

Romanian Christmas Carol

Lullaby for Christmas

Andante

Hungarian Christmas Carol

Little Brown Jug

Allegro

American Folk Song

Down Below in Bethlehem

Andante

Romanian Christmas Carol

The First Nowell

Andantino

Christmas Carol

March
(from "The Peasants' Cantata")

J.S.Bach

Little Rabbit

Romanian Children's Song

36

Intervals: the Third

High D and high E

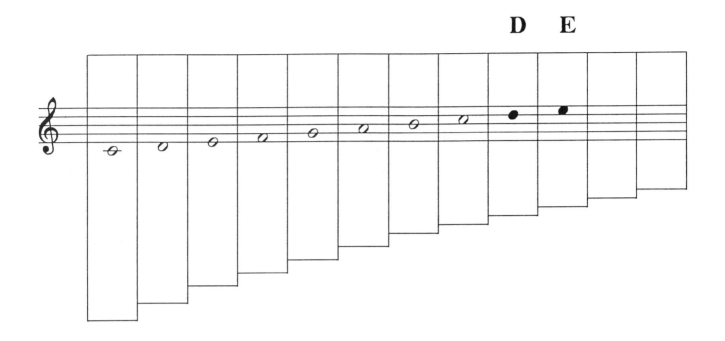

Studies

25

Andante

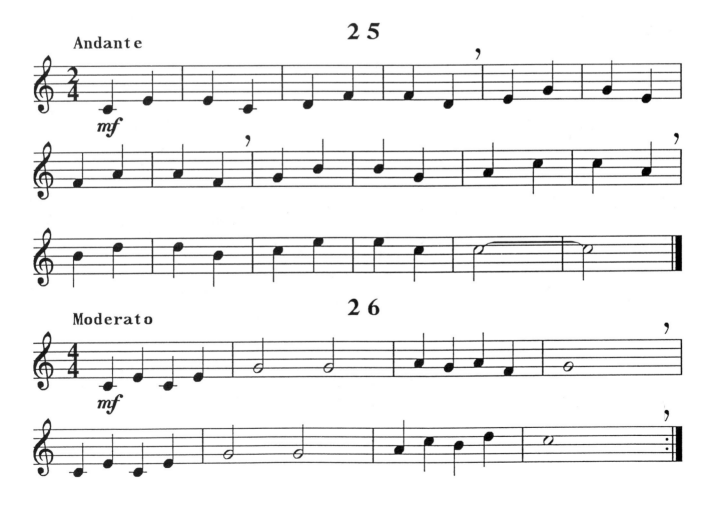

26

Moderato

Songs
Be Quiet Now

Andantino

Christmas Carol

Air

Andantino

W.A. Mozart

Hopping

Allegretto

C. Puscoiu

Oh, Susanna

American Folk Song

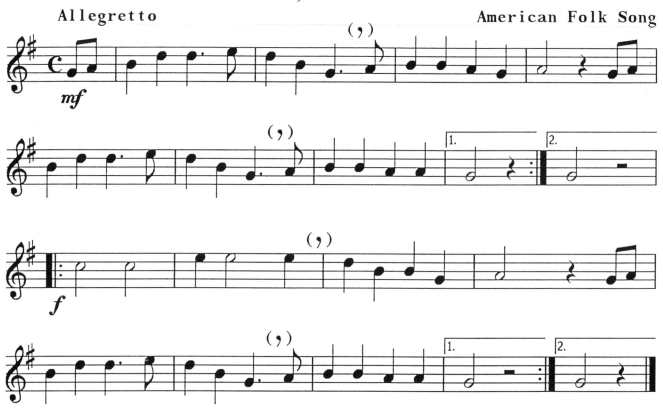

When the Saints Go Marching In

Spiritual

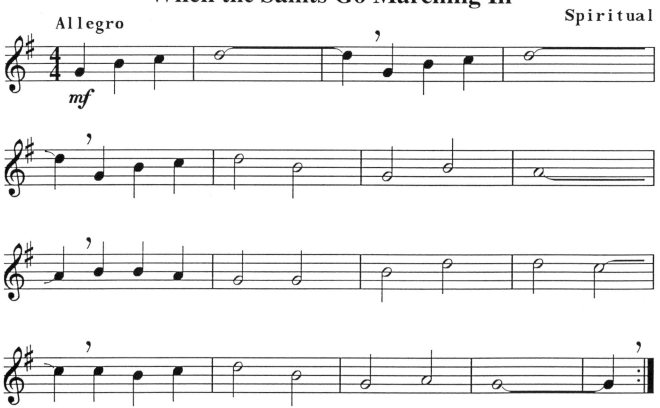

Auld Lang Syne

Dance from Brebu

41

A Child is Born

Fox, You Stole the Goose

Theme
(from "Swanlake")

Shepherd, Shepherd

Allegretto

Hungarian Christmas Carol

Thus the Good People Drink

Moderato

Romanian Folk Song

Angels and Shepherds

Allegretto

Czechian Christmas Carol

Chromatic Semitones

Until now we have studied what I call the diatonic pan flute and the only possibilities for playing were the keys of C major. To be able to extend our repertoire we have to learn to play chromatic semitones (sharps and flats), which is not an easy thing to do on the pan flute.

We can produce chromatic semitones on the pan flute by tilting the pan flute away from the player's body.

 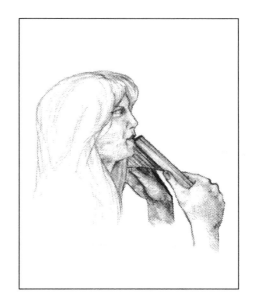

chromatic semitone

In the table below you can see which chromatic semitones can be played on each pipe of the pan flute.

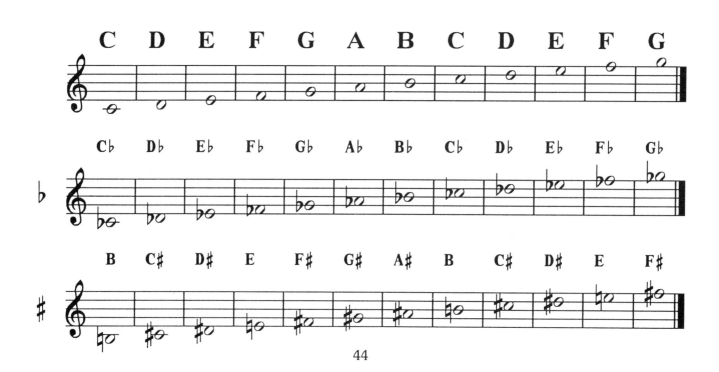

Studies

The angle of tilting the pan flutes should be about 30°, but it is not the same for all players and must be determined by listening until we get a chromatic tone of exactly a semitone. Because I want to indicate which tones are tilted I use an arrow above the note pointing downward. The angle of tilting is bigger in the lower register, and smaller in the higher register.

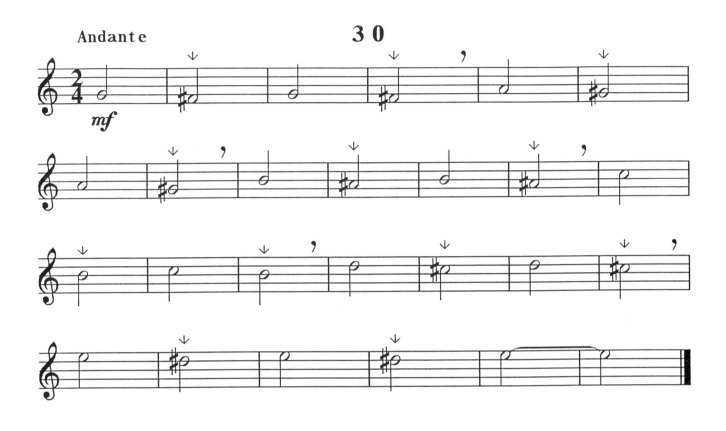

D.C. al Fine

Watch the key signature !

3 4

Fine

D.C. a Fine

35

Songs

Scarborough Fair

Traditional

God Rest Ye Merry, Gentlemen

English Carol

Andantino

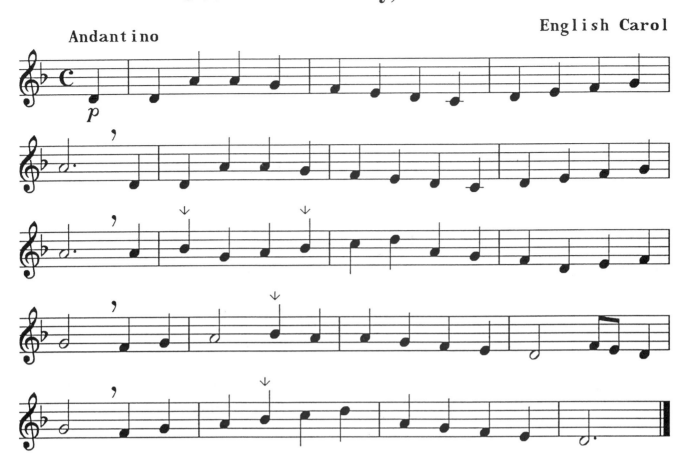

Aura Lee

Traditional

Andante

Melody

(from "Album for the Youth")

R. Schumann

Rondino

J. Ph. Rameau

Melody

Moderato

A. Rubinstein

Greensleeves

Andante

Old English Song

Fine

D.C. al Fine

Minuet

J.S. Bach

Romance

L. van Beethoven

Musette

J.S. Bach

Hava Naguila

Israeli Folk Song

Musz I Denn

Allegretto

German Folk Song

Intervals: the Fourth and Fifth

High F and High G

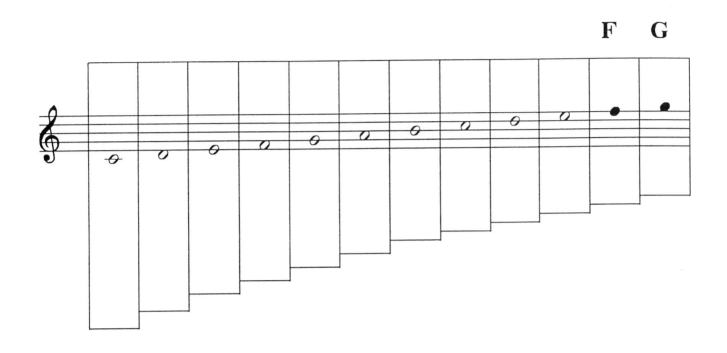

Studies

3 6

39 Allegretto

40 Andante

41 Moderato

Songs

London Bridge is Falling Down

O Come, All Ye Faithful

59

Song of the Volga Boatmen

Andante   Russian Folk Song

Gavotte

Andante   G.Fr. Handel

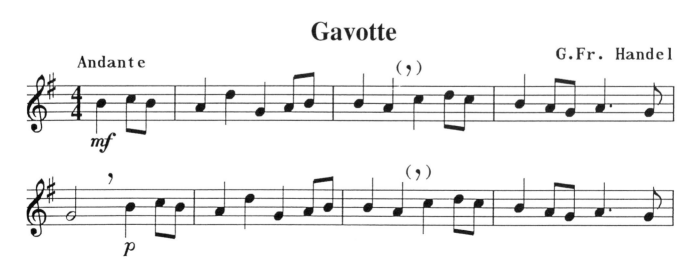

Merry Widow Waltz

F. Lehar

Sleep Well My Baby

Andante

Romanian Folk Song

Quadrille

Allegretto

J. Haydn

Tram, Take Me Home

Moderato

Romanian Folk Song

Gavotte

Andantino

G.Fr. Handel

Finale
(from Symphony no. 1)

Joh. Brahms

Theme
(from "Unfinished Symphony")

Fr. Schubert

Santa Lucia

Theme
(from "Eine kleine Nachtmusik")

We shall not practice especially in this book studies with intervals of a larger tone range: sixth, seventh and octave, because they are difficult for a beginning pan flutist. In the songs the sixth, seventh and octave appear a few times.

Staccato

Staccato is one of the most employed techniques in music and it exists on nearly all musical instruments. Staccato is symbolized by putting a dot over or under a note on the opposite side of the stem.

In practice staccato means starting a tone with a sharp attack of the tongue and the addition of a little accentuation, while the value of the note is shortened by half. Staccato is always used for short values of notes. On a pan flute there is only a slight difference between staccato and the normal attack of a tone, because in both cases the tongue is used.

Notation   Execution

To achieve a good staccato you move your tongue as when you are pronouncing the letter "t" (tu). The attack of the tone becomes more powerful and quicker than usual.

Studies

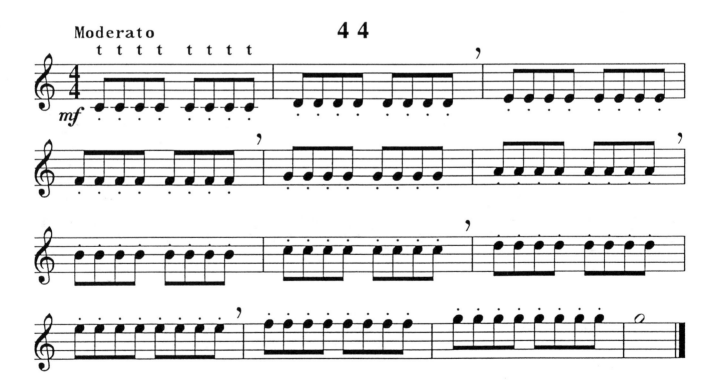

45

Allegretto

46

Allegro

simile (= the same, staccato)

47

Allegretto

simile

Songs

Burlesque
(from "Music Book for Wolfgang")

Allegro

L. Mozart

Andante

Andante

J. Haydn

She'll Be Coming Round the Mountain

I Have a Coin

Rondeau

Tambourin

Allegro

J.Ph. Rameau

Fine

D.C. al Fine

Gavotte

Allegretto

A. Corelli

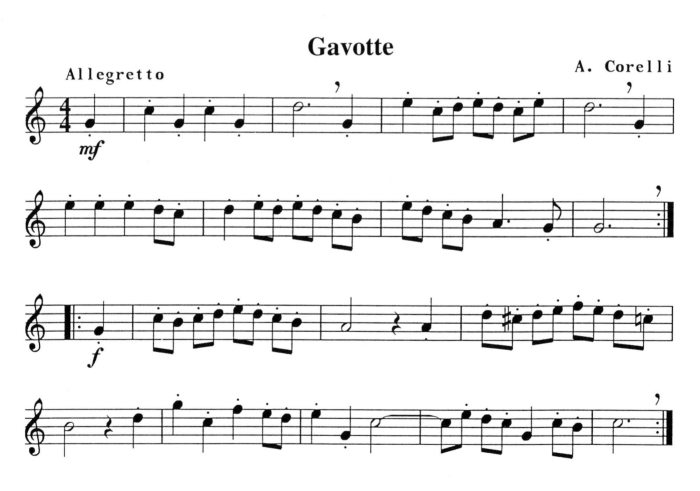

Can-Can

J. Offenbach

El Humahuaqueno

Bolivian Folk Song

German Dance

W.A. Mozart

El Cachimbo

Chilian Folk Song

72

Minuet

Martial Air

Galoppa, Galoppa

Chilian Folk Song

Legato

Legato (tying) is a special technique which is not used that often on the pan flute, because the way the instrument is built does not allow a proper use of this technical process.

Legato is possible between adjoining pipes diatonically in the way the pan flute is tuned. The first tone of a series is started off in the usual way. The next tones that are included under the legato mark are not attacked again. After the first tone is started the pan flute player keeps blowing. As he moves the instrument the pipes that follow provide the respective tones.

x = attack

Studies

48

Songs
Theme
(from "Moldavia")

B. Smetana

Gloria in Excelsis Deo

Christmas Carol

Theme
(from Sonatina)

L. van Beethoven

Humming Song

Allegretto

R. Schumann

Gavotte

Allegretto

J.S. Bach

Hark! The Herald Angels Sing

F. Mendelssohn

Long, Long Ago

Traditional

Melody

(from "Scheherazade")

N. Rimsky-Korsakow

Michael's Song

C. Puscoiu

Epilogue

I have now come to the end of this book and I hope the pan flute student has found it pleasant to use for practice. I am sure it was not always easy. This beginning is necessary for being able to practice music and to continue the study with other books and methods like my COMPLETE METHOD FOR PAN FLUTE. You can continue to learn with this method about vibrato, diatonic scales, arpeggios, ornaments, special effects, phrasing, how to use alto, tenor, bass or double bass pan flutes.

You can also continue to play pieces from the universal literature of music on my CLASSICAL REPERTOIRE FOR PAN FLUTE. You should keep increasing your musical baggage and perfect it. You should also broaden your skills in the area that holds your special interest: classical, folklore, light music, jazz, etc.

I wish you a lot of success !

Songs

Morning Has Broken

Allegretto

Traditional

Barbu The Fiddler

Andante

Romanian Folk Song

O Come, Emmanuel

Old Latin Song

Minuet

J. Krieger

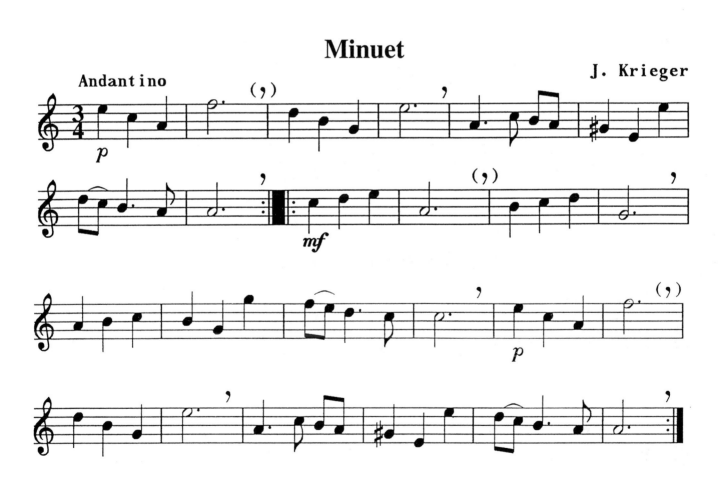

Plaisir d' Amour

J.P. Martini

The Yellow Rose of Texas

American Folk Song

Joy to the World

G.Fr. Handel

When I Was on Ialomita

Romanian Folk Song

Father Christmas

Romanian Christmas Carol

Silent Night

F.X. Gruber

March

(from "Judas Maccabaeus")

G.Fr. Handel

Lullaby

Joh. Brahms

Oh, My Darlin' Clementine

American Folk Song

Musette

J.S. Bach

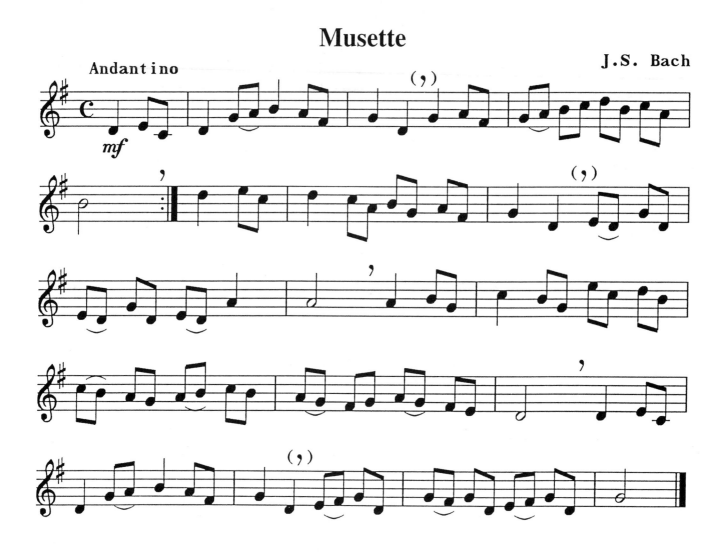

Amazing Grace

Traditional

Etude

Fr. Chopin

First Grief

R. Schumann

Theme
(from Symphony no. 40)

W.A. Mozart

La Cinquantaine

G. Marie

Three-leaved Clover

Romanian Folk Song

Gavotte

F.J. Gossec

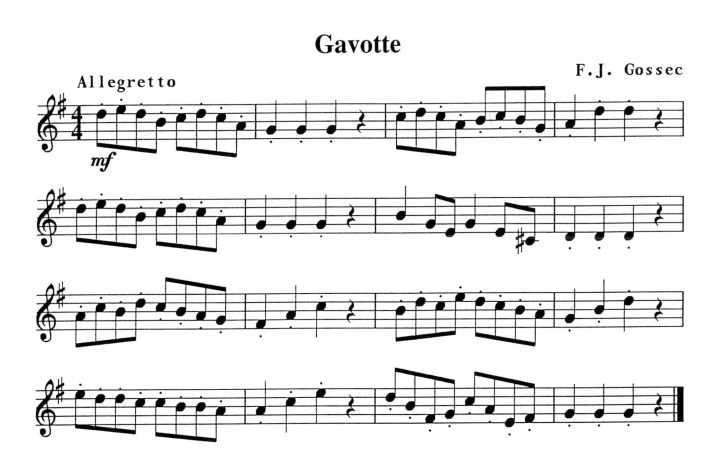

Early French Song

P.I. Tchaikovsky

Pavane

G. Fauré

O Sole Mio!

Andante
(from Violin Concerto)

F. Mendelssohn

Morning
(from "Peer Gynt")

E. Grieg

Air
(from Opera "The Magic Flute")
W.A. Mozart

Allegro

Melody

(from Piano Concerto no. 2)

S. Rachmaninoff